MAKERS AND TAKERS

Studying Food Webs in the Ocean

GWENDOLYN HOOKS

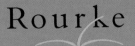

Rourke

Publishing LLC

Vero Beach, FL 32964
rourkepublishing.com

www.rourkepublishing.com

Project Assistance:
Also, the author thanks Dr. Michael Graham, Assistant Professor Moss Landing Marine Laboratories, San Jose State University, Julie Lundgren, and the team at Blue Door Publishing.

Photo credits:
Cover Images: Coral reef © Eldad Yitzhak, Shark © Ian Scott, Otter © Rui Manuel Teles Gomes, Sea Urchins © David Wilkins, Kelp © Paul Whitted Page 4 © Morozova Tatyana; Page 5 © Flominator; Page 6 © Stephan Kerkhofs; Page 7 © Galyna Andrushko, Flominator, Infrogmation, Morozova Tatyana; Page 8 © Valery Potapova; Page 9 © Ian Scott; Page 10 © Achim Raschka, NOAA; Page 11 © Liftarn; Page 12 © Paul Whitted; Page 13 © Valery Potapova; Page 14 © N Joy Neish; Page 15 © Brittany Courville; Page 17 © Brad Whitsitt; Page 18 © Brauer, A.; Page 19 © Paul Yates; Page 20 © Edgewater Media; Page 21 © Cory Smith; Page 22 © Rudyanto Wijaya; Page 23 © Annetje, Library Of Congress; Page 24 © NASA; Page 25 © Radim Spitzer; Page 26 © Dmitri Mihhailov, Juha Sompinmäki; Page 27 © Galina Barskaya, Valery Potapova; Page 29 © Ivan Cholakov

Editor: Jeanne Sturm

Cover and page design by Nicola Stratford, Blue Door Publishing

Library of Congress Cataloging-in-Publication Data

Hooks, Gwendolyn.
  Makers and takers : studying food webs in the ocean / Gwendolyn Hooks.
     p. cm. -- (Studying food webs)
  Includes index.
  ISBN 978-1-60472-319-9 (hardcover)
  ISBN 978-1-60472-784-5 (softcover)
  1. Marine ecology--Juvenile literature. 2. Food chains (Ecology)--Juvenile literature. I. Title.
  QH541.5.S3H66 2009
  577.7'16--dc22

Printed in the USA

CG/CG

Rourke Publishing

www.rourkepublishing.com – rourke@rourkepublishing.com
Post Office Box 3328, Vero Beach, FL 32964

Table Of Contents

Water Water Everywhere   4

Make It and Take It   12

Untangling the Web   16

Decomposers   24

Build, Build, Build   28

Glossary   30

Index   32

On The Cover

Tiger sharks prey on sea otters.

Sea otters eat sea urchins, crabs, clams, and octopuses.

Sea urchins eat plant and animal matter, including kelp.

Kelp provides food for ocean herbivores and omnivores.

Water Water Everywhere

Oceans may appear to be filled only with clear blue water, but they're brimming with life. Scientists believe there is more life in oceans than on land. Millions of plants, animals, and other **organisms** too tiny to see without special instruments live near the surface. One of the many organisms is phytoplankton. Since they are mainly one-celled organisms, they are not considered plants.

Small animals called zooplankton feed on phytoplankton. Some zooplankton are the larval form, or young form, of animals like crabs. Zooplankton can go through many different forms before they become adults.

CHEW ON THIS

Early explorers named the deepest ocean, Pacific, because it looked peaceful to them.

Without phytoplankton, ocean animals could not exist. Sometimes phytoplankton grows in such large numbers, satellites detect it from space.

Sweet As Honey

As phytoplankton float on the surface, they capture energy from sunlight and make glucose, which is a sugar. This is called **photosynthesis**. Marine animals eat glucose to survive. It's the same glucose people taste when eating honey or apples. The transfer of energy from the Sun to phytoplankton is the first link in the ocean's **food chain**. As animals eat phytoplankton, energy is transferred from plant to animal forming a second food chain link.

Octopuses eat shrimp, lobster, crab, and snails.

Energy transfer occurs any time an animal eats phytoplankton, plants, or animals. Each transfer links food together in a food chain. Ocean animals often eat more than one type of food. Some eat different foods at different stages of their life. This causes the food chain to branch off into a tangled web of eating and being eaten. Instead of a simple food chain, the transfer of energy is actually many chains interconnected into a **food web**.

CHEW ON THIS

If fishermen know where phytoplankton grow, they can cast their lines and reel in fish after fish.

An Ocean Food Chain

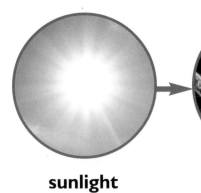

sunlight   **phytoplankton**   **zooplankton**   **fish**

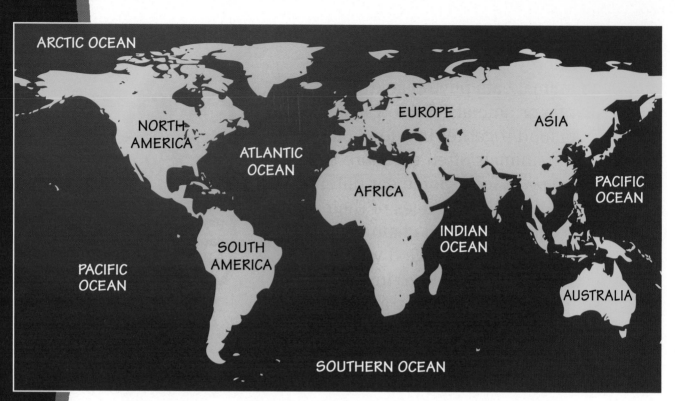

Oceans cover over 70 percent of the Earth's surface. They contain almost all of the water on the planet.

Water World

An **ecosystem** is a community of plants and animals that live in the same area. It also includes nonliving things like water and nutrients in the water. All ecosystems must have an energy source, usually the Sun. An ocean has many ecosystems. A coral reef is an ecosystem and a kelp forest is another. Animals that live on the ocean floor form still another ecosystem.

The Great Barrier Reef off the coast of
Australia is an ecosystem with 1,500 species
of fish and over 400 species of coral.

Super hot water escapes from deep beneath the ocean floor through volcanic openings called hydrothermal vents. Rich in minerals and bacteria, the water supports an ecosystem without photosynthesis. Instead, strange animals like tube worms, sea spiders, and squat lobsters rely on energy produced by bacteria in this deep, dark place.

Water emerges from a hydrothermal vent at temperatures ranging up to 400° C (725° F), compared to a typical 2° C (36° F) for the surrounding deep ocean water.

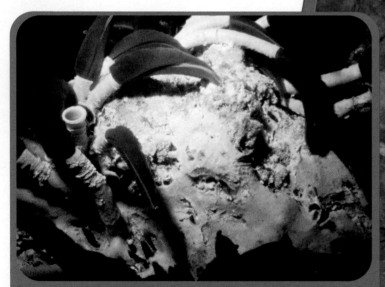

Encased in white tubes, tubeworms lurk on the bottom of the ocean.

On April 4, 1991, scientists aboard the submersible, Alvin, cruised toward a hydrothermal vent in the Pacific Ocean. They expected to find hoards of animals on the ocean floor. Instead, they found charred and dead tubeworms, mussels, and limpets. The deaths were the result of a volcano. The scientists called it Tubeworm Barbeque.

Make It and Take It

All ecosystems have makers and takers. Makers are called **primary producers** because they make, or produce, food for animals in the ecosystem. Consumers are the takers. They take, or consume, the food that is produced. A sea urchin munching on a blade of seaweed is an example of a producer and **primary consumer** relationship. The seaweed produces energy as food, and sea urchins consume it to live and grow. Crabs and fish eat the spiny sea urchins. They are **secondary consumers**.

CHEW ON THIS

Kelp can be added to ice cream to make it soft.

ARCTIC OCEAN

NORTH AMERICA

EUROPE

ATLANTIC OCEAN

PACIFIC OCEAN

AFRICA

* SOUTH AMERICA

★ = Galápagos Islands

SOUTHERN OCEAN

Marine biologist Michael Graham and his associates developed a computer program to locate underwater kelp forests. They used the program along with satellite reports and oceanographic instruments to help them find kelp forests near the Galapagos Islands. Galapagos kelp is on the threatened species list.

*Kelp is a primary producer. In some places kelp forests grow down 100 feet to 150 feet (30m to 45m) from the ocean surface. There are over 5,000 **species** of kelp.*

Only producers can make their own food. Everything else including blue whales, one of the largest animals in the ocean, depends on producers to survive, grow, and multiply. Some animals time their release of eggs to the growth cycles of marine plants. More plants grow in spring and summer when the temperatures are higher and sunlit days are longer. Sea grass, seaweed, and algae are the three types of producers.

Sea grasses are the only true plants in the ocean. Their roots take up nutrients necessary for producing flowers, pollen, fruits, and seeds. Sea grass leaves can be up to 3 feet (1m) long.

Algae also live in the ocean. Unlike sea grass, algae are not true plants. They don't have seeds or flowers. Rootless, algae absorb water all along their surface. Phytoplankton is a type of algae.

Seaweeds, a type of algae, grow in shallow water. Holdfasts hold them in place and keep them from floating away. Seaweed types include red, green, and brown. Kelp is large brown seaweed. But kelp is not completely brown. Its color ranges from brown to greenish brown.

Seaweed contains hollow, gas-filled structures called air bladders. These air bladders keep seaweed afloat so it can soak up the Sun's energy it needs for photosynthesis.

Untangling the Web

Scientists who study food webs place plants and animals in trophic or feeding levels. Plants are at the first, or bottom, level and are called autotrophs.

In the next level are **herbivores**, animals that eat plants. Copepods, relatives of shrimp and crabs, are in this second trophic level. Copepods are small, but some herbivores are larger, like snails and sea urchins that feed on kelp.

**killer
whales**

**seals,
sea lions, penguins**

swordfish, tuna, octopus

mackerel, herring, squid

copepod, moon snail, sea urchin, krill

phytoplankton, seaweed, sea grass

In an ecosystem, all organisms that feed on the same kind of food are in the same trophic level.

The next level includes mackerel, a fish that feeds on other small fish and krill, a type of zooplankton. Animals that feed on other animals are **carnivores**. As they feed, grow, and move about, they are eaten by larger animals.

It's lonely at the top. The top has fewer animals than the lower levels. Plants and phytoplankton can produce rapidly. But herbivores do not receive all of the energy produced by plants and phytoplankton. Some of the energy is lost. At each trophic level, less energy is received from the level below. That means there are fewer animals in the trophic levels at the top than at the bottom.

Ocean food webs can link to animals outside of the ocean. Pelicans dive for fish and some fish leap out of the water to catch low-flying insects.

Marine animals feed in one of five ways. Grazers are the herbivores that consume plants. **Predators** hunt, or prey, on other animals. **Scavengers** search for dead animals. Filter feeders like barnacles, oysters, and clams sift food out of the water as it flows by them. Deposit feeders ingest, or take in, muddy sediment and extract, or take out, food that is mixed with the mud.

Some deep sea angler fish dangle a light that looks like a tasty snack. Any critter attempting to eat it becomes the snack!

Gooseneck barnacles filter food with their feathery legs.

CHEW ON THIS

Some marine biologists study marine ecology. They want to learn more about ocean food webs, animal and plant behavior, how fish communicate, and how human behavior affects ocean life.

Food webs diagram the movement of energy from plants to animals and from animals to animals. Animals do not keep all of the incoming energy. Some energy is used as they move about, just as people use energy when they walk and run. Less energy is available as it moves up the food chain, so there are fewer animals at the top. There are fewer whales and great white sharks at the top of the food chain than the millions of phytoplankton at the bottom.

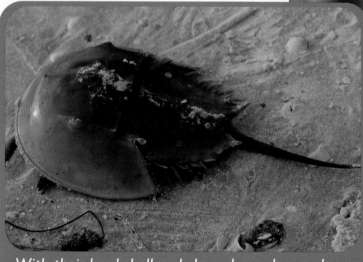

With their hard shell and claws, horseshoe crabs look like other crabs, but are related to scorpions and spiders.

Sharks, with their rows of sharp
teeth, are fearsome predators.

Getting Your Hands Wet

The more oceanographers study the ocean, the more they learn about food webs. Some oceanographers spend months aboard research ships, working 18-20 hours each day. They dive in submersibles to study containers of chemical and radioactive wastes that have been dumped into the ocean. They want to know what effect the content of these containers has had on ocean life.

Oceanographers sample water to determine its salt content and temperature. They also measure the amount of available light at different depths of the ocean. Studying deep ocean life is difficult because most animals will die once they are brought to the surface. Oceanographers work hard to discover ways to keep them alive. Still others work in laboratories analyzing the data, or information, brought to them.

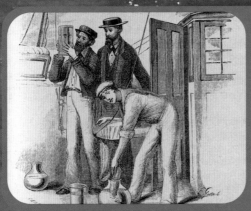

The four-year voyage (1872 to 1876) of the British ship H.M.S. Challenger is considered the beginning of oceanography. During the voyage, many new species of plants and animals were discovered and underwater mountains were mapped. This drawing shows three men on the deck of the H.M.S. Challenger studying jellyfish.

Oceanographers often find themselves face to face with the plants and animals they study.

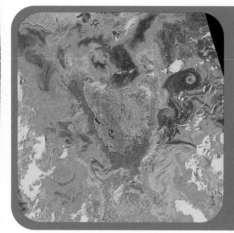

A satellite image can show high concentration of phytoplankton. Instead of spending weeks collecting data, satellites quickly provide the information for researchers. The red and orange colors in this satellite photo indicate high levels of phytoplankton.

Decomposers

Bacteria are organisms that thrive almost anywhere, even in the ocean. They are found on dead things, living things, in sediment, and on the ocean floor. Some types of bacteria just float in the water.

Bacteria are important to ocean ecosystems because they are **decomposers**. They break down dead plants and dead animals into nutrients. Phytoplankton absorb these nutrients and start the cycle of photosynthesis once again. Decomposers are a vital link in the ocean's food webs. Without them, plants could not photosynthesize. Then ecosystems would be destroyed.

CHEW ON THIS

Bone is one of the hardest animal parts to decompose.

Up It Comes

Upwelling is the slow rise of nutrient rich water toward the sunlit ocean surface. Waves, wind, and ocean currents cause the upward movement of the water. Many of the small animals that feed on phytoplankton time their egg laying to the surge in phytoplankton caused by upwelling.

The upwelling of nutrients feeds phytoplankton, just as fertilizer feeds lawns.

BROKEN LINKS!

Using a beach as a garbage dump is life-threatening for the animals that live near the coast. Some beaches have been closed because the pollution is harmful to people.

Most oil spills occur as oil is being transported from oil fields to where it is refined or consumed. Wind and ocean currents help spread the oil across the ocean surface. In water along the coasts, oil smothers or poisons the plants and animals that live in the coastal ecosystems. Oil spills in open water are less of a problem. As the oil spills, it disperses in the water and becomes less toxic, or poisonous.

City waste called sewage is partly made up of excrement. Excrement is the waste product that leaves our bodies. If untreated sewage is pumped into coastal water, it can have long lasting and severe effects even on bottom fish. Sometimes it results in diseases like black gill and fin rot. Some kelp forests off the coast of California have been destroyed by waste products. This destroyed the habitats of fish and shellfish that depended on the kelp.

When people add or take away something from an ocean's ecosystem it changes the natural levels of plants, animals, or nutrients. This causes the ecosystem to become **polluted**.

The Indian Ocean is home to over 11,000 species of plants and animals. More than 70 percent of marine turtles nest along its beaches. Because of destructive fishing practices and untreated sewage, the Indian Ocean is suffering.

Build, Build, Build

Each year, more and more coastlines are developed into housing complexes, shopping areas, tourist attractions, gas stations, parking lots, and industrial complexes. Along with the buildings come the people who will live, work, and vacation there. To protect people and their property from erosion and storm damage, seawalls are constructed.

Soon the coast has changed and the original beach is no longer the beautiful, sandy beach that once attracted so many people. Pollution caused by littering and dredging has changed the way it once looked and changed the ecosystems that once thrived there.

In spite of the negative changes, there are many ways to make a difference.

- Leave aquatic plants and animals where you find them.
- Don't upset ecosystems by returning aquarium fish to the ocean.
- If you live near a coastal area, organize a "Beach Clean Up Day".
- Become a steward or keeper of the environment and recycle everything you can.

A better environment starts with one person leading and inspiring others to follow.

Scientific organizations like the National Ocean Service serve to preserve and enhance the ocean's natural resources and ecosystems. Along with local governments and the public, they reverse the damage caused by pollution. They also work to protect the oceans and their many plants and animals for the enjoyment of all.

The National Ocean Service is studying the red and white striped lionfish. Once located only in the Pacific Ocean, now scientists find them off the coast of Georgia.

Glossary

carnivores (KAR-nuh-vorz): animals that eat other animals

decomposers (dee-cum-POH-zerz): animals or plants that break down other plants and animals into nutrients

ecosystem (EE-koh-sis-tum): the relationships between all the plants and animals and the place in which they live

food chain (FOOD CHAYN): a series of plants and animals, each of which is eaten by the one after it

food web (FOOD WEHB): in an ecosystem, the intricate network of food chains

herbivores (HER-bi-vorz): animals that feed on plants and phytoplankton

organisms (OR-guh-niz-uhmz): living plants and animals

photosynthesis (foh-toh-SIN-thuh-siss): the process by which green plants transform the Sun's energy into food

polluted (puh-loo-ted): when the natural levels of plants and animals have been changed, destroying them in the process

predators (PRED-uh-turz): animals that hunt other animals for food

primary consumer(s) (PRYE-mair-ee kuhn-SOO-murz): herbivores, the animals that eat plants and phytoplankton

primary producers (PRYE-mair-ee Proh-DOOS-serz): plants and phytoplankton that that perform photosynthesis

scavengers (SKAV-uhn-jerz): animals that eat dead animals

secondary consumers (SEHK-uhn-dair-ee kuhn-SOO-murz): animals that eat herbivores

species (SPEE-sheez or SPEE-seez): members of the same animal or plant family

Further Reading

Want to learn more about ocean food webs? The following books and websites are a great place to start.

Books

Berger, Melvin and Gilda Berger. *Sharks and Other Wild Water Animals.* Cartwheel Books, 2006.

Crawley, Annie. *Ocean Life From A to Z and DVD.* Reader's Digest, 2007.

Fleisher, Paul. *Ocean Food Webs.* Lerner Publications, 2007.

Websites

National Ocean Service
http://oceanservice.noaa.gov/education/welcome.html

Secrets of the Ocean Realm
http://www.pbs.org/oceanrealm/

Exploring the Oceans
http://www.mos.org/oceans/scientist/index.html

Index

autotrophs   16

carnivores   17

decomposers   24

deposit feeders   18

filter feeders   18

food chain   6, 7, 20

grazers   18

herbivores   16, 17, 18

kelp   8, 12, 13, 15, 16, 27

oceanographers   22, 23

photosynthesis   6, 10, 24

pollution   26, 28, 29

primary consumers   12

primary producers   12

predators   18, 21

prey   18

scavengers   18

secondary consumers   12

trophic   16, 17

zooplankton   4, 7

About the Author

Gwendolyn Hooks has been an avid reader all of her life. When she was a child and supposed to be asleep, Gwendolyn sat by her window and used the streetlight to read "just one more chapter." Gwendolyn graduated from the University of Missouri-St. Louis with an education degree. Still an avid reader, she now writes fiction and nonfiction for children. This is her seventh book for young readers. She has three adult children and lives in Oklahoma City with her husband.